The Poetry of Flowers

Published by Photo Accents/CR Enterprises (New York), LLC
www.photo-accents.com

Design: Camille Rankin

ISBN: 978-0-578-08677-4

Printed in China

The Poetry of Flowers

❀

Edited and with photography by Camille Rankin

Published by Photo Accents
New York City

From **Flowers, by Henry Wadsworth Longfellow**

In all places, then, and in all seasons,
Flowers expand their light and soul-like wings,
Teaching us, by most persuasive reasons,
How akin they are to human things.

And with childlike, credulous affection
We behold their tender buds expand;
Emblems of our own great resurrection,
Emblems of the bright and better land.

Sonnet 94, by William Shakespeare

They that have power to hurt and will do none,
That do not do the thing they most do show,
Who, moving others, are themselves as stone,
Unmoved, cold, and to temptation slow;
They rightly do inherit heaven's graces
And husband nature's riches from expense;
They are the lords and owners of their faces,
Others but stewards of their excellence.
The summer's flower is to the summer sweet,
Though to itself it only live and die,
But if that flower with base infection meet,
The basest weed outbraves his dignity:
For sweetest things turn sourest by their deeds;
Lilies that fester smell far worse than weeds.

My Pretty Rose Tree, by William Blake

A flower was offered to me:
Such a flower as May never bore.
But I said "I've a Pretty Rose-tree,"
And I passed the sweet flower o'er.

Then I went to my Pretty Rose-tree:
To tend her by day and by night.
But my Rose turn'd away with jealousy:
And her thorns were my only delight.

I Wandered Lonely as a Cloud, by William Wordsworth

I wandered lonely as a cloud
That floats on high o'er vales and hills,
When all at once I saw a crowd,
A host, of golden daffodils;
Beside the lake, beneath the trees,
Fluttering and dancing in the breeze.

Continuous as the stars that shine
And twinkle on the milky way,
They stretched in never-ending line
Along the margin of a bay:
Ten thousand saw I at a glance,
Tossing their heads in sprightly dance.

The waves beside them danced; but they
Out-did the sparkling waves in glee:
A poet could not but be gay,
In such a jocund company:
I gazed—and gazed—but little thought
What wealth the show to me had brought:

For oft, when on my couch I lie
In vacant or in pensive mood,
They flash upon that inward eye
Which is the bliss of solitude;
And then my heart with pleasure fills,
And dances with the daffodils.

Buddhist Sutra

As a flower that is lovely,
Colourful, and fragrant
Even so fruitful is the well-spoken word
Of one who practices it.

As from a heap of flowers
Many kinds of garlands can be made,
So many good deeds should be done
By one born a mortal.

The perfume of flower blows not against the wind,
Nor does the fragrance of sandal-wood, tagara and jasmine,
But the fragrance of the virtuous blows against the wind.
The virtuous man pervades all direction.

Afternoon on a Hill, by Edna St. Vincent Millay

I will be the gladdest thing
    Under the sun!
I will touch a hundred flowers
    And not pick one.

I will look at cliffs and clouds
    With quiet eyes,
Watch the wind bow down the grass,
    And the grass rise.

And when lights begin to show
    Up from the town,
I will mark which must be mine,
    And then start down!

The Last Chrysanthemum, by Thomas Hardy

Why should this flower delay so long
　　To show its tremulous plumes?
Now is the time of plaintive robin-song,
　　When flowers are in their tombs.

Through the slow summer, when the sun
　　Called to each frond and whorl
That all he could for flowers was being done,
　　Why did it not uncurl?

It must have felt that fervid call
　　Although it took no heed,
Waking but now, when leaves like corpses fall,
　　And saps all retrocede.

Too late its beauty, lonely thing,
　　The season's shine is spent,
Nothing remains for it but shivering
　　In tempests turbulent.

Had it a reason for delay,
　　Dreaming in witlessness
That for a bloom so delicately gay
　　Winter would stay its stress?

I talk as if the thing were born
　　With sense to work its mind;
Yet it is but one mask of many worn
　　By the Great Face behind.

The Flowers, by Robert Louis Stevenson

All the names I know from nurse:
Gardener's garters, Shepherd's purse,
Bachelor's buttons, Lady's smock,
And the Lady Hollyhock.

Fairy places, fairy things,
Fairy woods where the wild bee wings,
Tiny trees for tiny dames—
These must all be fairy names!

Tiny woods below whose boughs
Shady fairies weave a house;
Tiny tree-tops, rose or thyme,
Where the braver fairies climb!

Fair are grown-up people's trees,
But the fairest woods are these;
Where, if I were not so tall,
I should live for good and all.

from **Dahlia in the Window, by Caroline Misner**

Pale and translucent as pink lemonade,
the morning sun filtered its petals
to pure lightness;

a saffron haze
near the stem, pallid fuchsia at its tips,
it yawns, unfurling its petals into
the summer air laden with mist
and amber seed.

As if some little Arctic flower, by Emily Dickinson

As if some little Arctic flower
Upon the polar hem—
Went wandering down the Latitudes
Until it puzzled came
To continents of summer—
To firmaments of sun—
To strange, bright crowds of flowers—
And birds, of foreign tongue!
I say, As if this little flower
To Eden, wandered in—
What then? Why nothing,
Only, your inference therefrom!

Eutopia, by Francis Turner Palgrave

There is a garden where lilies
And roses are side by side;
And all day between them in silence
The silken butterflies glide.

I may not enter the garden,
Though I know the road thereto;
And morn by morn to the gateway
I see the children go.

They bring back light on their faces;
But they cannot bring back to me
What the lilies say to the roses,
Or the songs of the butterflies be.

Love's Rose, by Percy Bysshe Shelley

1.

Hopes that swell in youthful breasts,
Live not through the waste of time!
Love's rose a host of thorns invests;
Cold, ungenial is the clime,
Where its honours blow.
Youth says, The purple flowers are mine,
Which die the while they glow.

2.

Dear the boon to Fancy given,
Retracted whilst it's granted:
Sweet the rose which lives in Heaven
Although on earth 'tis planted,
Where its honours blow,
While by earth's slaves the leaves are riven
Which die the while they glow.

3.

Age cannot Love destroy,
But Perfidy can blast the flower,
Even when in most unwary hour
It blooms in Fancy's bower.
Age cannot Love destroy,
But Perfidy can rend the shrine
In which its vermeil splendours shine.

from **Endymion, by John Keats**

A thing of beauty is a joy for ever:
Its loveliness increases; it will never
Pass into nothingness; but still will keep
A bower quiet for us, and a sleep
Full of sweet dreams, and health, and quiet breathing.
Therefore, on every morrow, are we wreathing
A flowery band to bind us to the earth,
Spite of despondence, of the inhuman dearth
Of noble natures, of the gloomy days,
Of all the unhealthy and o'er-darkened ways
Made for our searching: yes, in spite of all,
Some shape of beauty moves away the pall
From our dark spirits. Such the sun, the moon,
Trees old and young, sprouting a shady boon
For simple sheep; and such are daffodils
With the green world they live in; and clear rills
That for themselves a cooling covert make
'Gainst the hot season; the mid forest brake,
Rich with a sprinkling of fair musk-rose blooms:
And such too is the grandeur of the dooms
We have imagined for the mighty dead;
All lovely tales that we have heard or read:
An endless fountain of immortal drink,
Pouring unto us from the heaven's brink.

Flower in the Crannied Wall,
by Alfred, Lord Tennyson

Flower in the crannied wall,
I pluck you out of the crannies,
I hold you here, root and all, in my hand,
Little flower—but if I could understand
What you are, root and all, all in all,
I should know what God and man is.

Let It Be Forgotten, by Sara Teasdale

Let it be forgotten, as a flower is forgotten,
    Forgotten as a fire that once was singing gold,
Let it be forgotten for ever and ever,
    Time is a kind friend, he will make us old.

If anyone asks, say it was forgotten
    Long and long ago,
As a flower, as a fire, as a hushed footfall
    In a long forgotten snow.
This is wisdom which man must learn.

Hugo's "flower to butterfly," by Eugene Field

Sweet, bide with me and let my love
Be an enduring tether;
Oh, wanton not from spot to spot,
But let us dwell together.

You've come each morn to sip the sweets
With which you found me dripping,
Yet never knew it was not dew
But tears that you were sipping.

You gambol over honey meads
Where siren bees are humming;
But mine the fate to watch and wait
For my beloved's coming.

The sunshine that delights you now
Shall fade to darkness gloomy;
You should not fear if, biding here,
You nestled closer to me.

So rest you, love, and be my love,
That my enraptured blooming
May fill your sight with tender light,
Your wings with sweet perfuming.

Or, if you will not bide with me
Upon this quiet heather,
Oh, give me wing, thou beauteous thing,
That we may soar together.

Tulips, by A.E. Stallings

The tulips make me want to paint,
Something about the way they drop
Their petals on the tabletop
And do not wilt so much as faint,

Something about their burnt-out hearts,
Something about their pallid stems
Wearing decay like diadems,
Parading finishes like starts,

Something about the way they twist
As if to catch the last applause,
And drink the moment through long straws,
And how, tomorrow, they'll be missed.

The way they're somehow getting clearer,
The tulips make me want to see—
The tulips make the other me
(The backwards one who's in the mirror,

The one who can't tell left from right),
Glance now over the wrong shoulder
To watch them get a little older
And give themselves up to the light.

Ah! Sunflower, by William Blake

Ah! Sunflower, weary of time.
Who countest the steps of the Sun;
Seeking after that sweet golden clime
Where the traveller's journey is done.

Where the Youth pined away with desire,
And the pale Virgin shrouded in snow:
Arise from their graves and aspire.
Where my Sunflower wishes to go.

Sonnet 44, by Elizabeth Barrett Browning

Beloved, thou hast brought me many flowers
Plucked in the garden, all the summer through
And winter, and it seemed as if they grew
In this close room, nor missed the sun and showers.
So, in the like name of that love of ours,
Take back these thoughts which here unfolded too,
And which on warm and cold days I withdrew
From my heart's ground. Indeed, those beds and bowers
Be overgrown with bitter weeds and rue,
And wait thy weeding; yet here's eglantine,
Here's ivy!—take them, as I used to do
Thy flowers, and keep them where they shall not pine.
Instruct thine eyes to keep their colors true,
And tell thy soul their roots are left in mine.

from **If You Forget Me, by Pablo Neruda**

If suddenly
you forget me
do not look for me,
for I shall already have forgotten you....

But
if each day,
each hour,
you feel that you are destined for me
with implacable sweetness,
if each day a flower
climbs up to your lips to seek me,
ah my love, ah my own,
in me all that fire is repeated,
in me nothing is extinguished or forgotten,
my love feeds on your love, beloved,
and as long as you live it will be in your arms
without leaving mine.

THIS BOOK IS DEDICATED TO MY MOTHER, WITH LOVE

ACKNOWLEDGMENTS

"Afternoon on a Hill" © 1917, 1945 by Edna St. Vincent Millay.

"Dahlia in the Window," by Caroline Misner, first appeared in *The Litchfield Review,* Vol. 3, No. 4, Winter 2006. Reprinted by permission of the author.

"Tulips," by A.E. Stallings, first appeared in *Poetry* magazine in 2009 and will appear in the forthcoming book OLIVES, from Northwestern University Press. Reprinted by permission of the author.

"If You Forget Me," by Pablo Neruda, translated by Donald D. Walsh, from THE CAPTAIN'S VERSES, copyright ©1972 by Pablo Neruda and Donald D. Walsh. Reprinted by permission of New Directions Publishing Corp.